FOUR POETS

FOUR POETS

First published in the United Kingdom in 2024 by
The Choir Press
In conjunction with Beckit Books

ISBN 978-1-78963-444-0

Introduction

Maggie, Bill, Sarah and Barry first read together at a *Roundabout Nights* event which took place at a *Colony* exhibition at The Halpern Gallery in October 2018. This reading was a huge success and the four poets agreed to read together again.

In 2023, as part of the Rainham Poetry Festival, in association with Medway River Lit, Maggie, Bill, Sarah and Barry are re-uniting for a reading. To commemorate this event Beckit Books are proud to publish a book containing a sample of poetry from each of these four outstanding poets.

Contents **Page**

Maggie Harris

Maggie Harris was born in Guyana and lives in the UK. She has published ten books of poetry, prose and a memoir, Kiskadee Girl. Awards include The Guyana Prize for Literature, The Commonwealth Short Story Prize and The Wales Poetry Award.

The Word

on carrying the word from guyana to london i stumbled
fled anansi arachne daffodils how now brown cow what if
on carrying the word from bridgetown to castries i fell
partook of the fruit of the manchineel tree
felt the word swell in my throat   swallowed
and carried on   on carrying the word i was abused
ignored some laughed some scorned   my teeth,
skin, clothes, hair   the amble in my rhythm
the universe of my influence
the fashioning of my words
the untuned cadence
the ripple of middle passages
the roar of middle passages
the fertile ground of middle passages
the bright souls of middle passages
the storm   some, not all, missed the fact
that words sail on the wind
and only lodge in deep coves, quiet streams
the pauses of travellers
so hear me now   this word
this word in every stumble   each push back
it rises and carries on   from guyana to london
to broadstairs barbados st lucia   cumbria ireland
to wales portugal   havana   goa
to you

Anansi Hit Broadstairs

An ode to Broadstairs Folk Week

Anansi hit Broadstairs
All eight feet ringing with bells
A yellow tam pon he dreads
Scuttle down the High Street
Checking out The Albert, The Rose
The garden at Bombers
Then down through the York Gate
Slide in the Tartar Frigate.
He buying a pint and question the landlord –
Seh man, I hear something call Folk Week does happen here
You have my brudders from Africa, Ireland and Hingland
Causing hurricane; djembe and clogs, morris and fiddlers
Jamming up the town wicked to Kingdom come!?
Man, I ketch boat, bus and plane to land here
But the place so quiet!
Is only sea I hearing – tell me, is lie they lie 'bout
Multiculture and Torchlight Procession?
The landlord give Anansi another pint and say,
Mate you late! Folk Week was last week!
But those who know Anansi know
he always got the last word –
Brud, no way Anansi late! Anansi come early,
ready for next year!

Migrant Woman Bodysong

This is the shape of my country she said

and she trailed her finger from the sky of

her brow to her throat where the pulse beat

its heartime. This is the shape of my

country she said and we climbed the

ridges of the Pakoraima Mountains

whose chill made peaks

of her nipples. This is the shape

of my country she said and we wandered

the plains where the Rupununi savannahed her

belly. This is the shape of my country she said

and dipped her fingers in rivers where otter

smells dampened and lingered. This is the

shape of my cunt

ry she said

and i lost my way

and ilostmyway

in her forest.

Barbados

for George Lamming and Kamau Brathwaite

Barbados, where my soul fathers divined the dance
Colour my soul with the light of wisdom
Old men on the hill, travel my limestone arteries
Our breath so near, so far from Africa
Call my mothers in from the shores
Usher the songs, the singers, the writers
Innovations and reverberations rippling
From the drum to the pen. My mouth does not tire
Of syllables, remind me again and again
How we can build castles out of sand, and that
We are siblings under our skins.

Chillenden

Outlined against the skyline, blue
T-shirt, hair scraped back
Tall, golden corn
We had scythed our way through calm countryside
Flat fields raked with ditches
Poppies on the banks
Stiles low enough for our daughter to clamber
Green blackberries, skewiff hedges
In the distance, the windmill
This is where they found them, hacked
Beneath a tree, mother, daughter, dog too
I hide the photo. Can never return.

Paradise Fruit

St Lucia?
Walcott drew me there, essays later.
Fretwork balconies, the boy returning,
Anna, Castries burning.

We found the beach near Cap Estate
the tropical dream, surf pounding
wide-leafed trees who dropped
their golden fruit of topaz.

I am not a tourist. I
am a Guyana woman re-emerging.
Here, I tell my lover and my child
y'all try this, dounze from back home

we had a tree big big by we back door.
I take the first bite, palms
and jewels glinting, say, is all right
this is Paradise, and from up high

birds laughed and cracked their beaks
on bark where loose messages flap
Do Not Sit Beneath Do Not Eat.
Our mouths began to burn.

Shame drops through my bones.
I am become Snow White's mother.
Eve.   Take this, here is my body. Eat.

From Gros Islet to Castries Hospital
Francis the taxi driver reassures us
no-one's died. Ushers us
through patients waiting, heads curled

like question marks round doorways
incredulous at tourists
eating manchineel.

My daughter's screams are louder than the surf
rivalling the scratching of this poet's pen.
Is it a folly then, this tale, these words
that fashion beauty out of pain?

Extract from **Havana**

Havana *I dreamed you ...*

... skin peeling
Conquistador-gold, cupolas
columns, colonnades

cutting long shadows
on cobbles. Dogs hound the cool
of stone, the Gothic doorways

where Moorish oases
date palms and fountains
beckon

through a door frame
an old man's bed

his thin feet rest
on cardboard rescued
from the street

the courtyard of The Valencia Hotel
a gardener drenches the crotons
from a dented watering can
the yucca and the ginger-lily
wait   water runs on the tiles
green-blazered waiters
ease platters between
red elbows

and the curl
of black
wrought iron

the Cuban store for Cubans
shelves bare of milk powder
rationed bread, rice, black beans

and hunger meets in a place
patrolled by the guards
dressed in that particular green

favoured by revolutionaries

I walk, past clapped-out cars
plaster-dust and rubble
four centuries tired of standing

Havana I dream you.

The Lake Hotel, Killarney

This time it's raining and I am still a swift
borne in on the currents of the Atlantic stream.
This is still Lough Leane and the castle ruins
still an island in a sea of green.
A pair of mute swans are still here
on the rain-whipped waves, although
the heron is not.
We are still not amongst those who can
afford to stay,
but elegance and the view is ours for the price
of Guinness or coffee in the Punch Bowl tavern.
The salmon and the trout still hang on the wall
staring through glazed eyes to the lake
where a couple in black have left the terrace
to follow the spell of water. The chairs
are still upended, holding to the promise of rain
and we're all on a ship on a sea of flight
and you'll see them all if you visit at night
with their gowns and gloves, and twice-shone
shoes gliding along the terrace
while the men discuss the price of war
with one more drink at the bar.
But it takes a poet to stitch them in, from one century
to another; and wonder if our souls will wander
anywhere we find water.

GOA

I belong in a garden like this
fairy lights strung tree to tree

candles flickering like nymphs
bats streaming overhead

we scan the menu in the half light
waiters flit between the tables

and the bare shoulders of women
who have spent all day at the beach

I belong in a garden like this
the sea a whisper away
keeping the secrets of my kin

who sailed from Portuguese shores
to worship here in houses of dark wood
at altars with silver candlesticks

Outside this ring of trees scooters whizz
all day and night
streets throng with the children of de Gama
four strong on pillion

stalls bow with gold and tin
leather and plastic
melon juices spill on the bare feet of the woman
begging for rupees

but the bats are here elemental
mythic
owning the blackness of caves where souls dwell
their accusatory fingers of flight.

Island

You always dream of places
where no human voice breaks the landscape
high clifftops, crags, bare estuaries
that are not bare at all but brimming
at their waterlines with skewers, egrets
migrants like human souls seeking
resting place after resting place.
I teased you that no man is an island
we need to seek the sound of voices, warmth
to hold the fear, the echo, close
keep the sun at east or west
watch the shadow.
Only now I know your dreaming
shares the source, the wide sweep of land
the cries of seabirds
the stillness of a Cumbrian lake.
Now I know, now I know
it is I who feared the loneliness of coves
the surge of empty bays
that small i in islands.
Come, help me build a causeway
here, now.

Lake Christmas

That Christmas, we took to the fells, anointed ourselves
in its waters, understood the blessing was to be there at all

As travellers, we were one short; her absence
had initiated our presence there, sent us reeling

four hundred motorway miles through blizzards
seeking a solace only to be found amongst great
depths and heights

The owner of the cottage loaned us a plastic Christmas tree
which leaned absurdly against a windowpane
struggling against its inability to frame

Derwentwater, substituted chintz.

On Boxing Day it rained. We watched
the brave backpack their children up Cat Bells
in bright yellow waterproofs

that took me back to Berbice where snorkelled
yellow-clad workers sprayed mosquito larvae
in the grass around our school

We made the best of things; worked at our delight at being there
stopping the car above Bassentwaite to contemplate

that still, yet undulating place whose beauty leaves a residue
that scratches at the arteries and mixes metaphors,
joy and pain

These years on I struggle still to redefine that Christmas
that urge to celebrate a birth whilst drowning
both in beauty, and amniotic symmetry.

Cwmpengraig, Place of Stones

Where yuh navel string bury is not necessarily home
This gurl gon walk my grandmother say
And walk I walk from Guyana to West Wales
And leave I leave that place of oceans and slave bones
For bruk down cottages where people still pray

And come I come with my forked tongue split syntax
Of Hinglish and street Creole to wander lanes
With no names and no map where even
Sat nav wuk hard to find being alimbo
Beyond satellite beyond stars

And stars and dreams of stars and songs called
These Welsh from home
To cross oceans to a continent of the imagination
And is peel this country peel like onion, garden
Cups my cottage

In its fists of seasons, caring nothing for my ignorance
Of names, pronunciation, language

And History running in the stream right there
Beneath the stone: millworker foot-bottom still indent
Ghost voice talking story wild a catchafire
How he catching boat with intention get the hell
Outa dis place

It nat fuh him to know some gurl would bring
His story right back here
And tell him tales of sugarcane and captains

Tracing latitude and longitude
With quadrant, quill and octopus ink
Is laugh he would laugh true true
Whilst that stream keep gurgling
Stones keep tumbling
Underscore the footfall of my feet.

Note: This poem is also translated into Welsh by Welsh poet Menna Elfyn.

The Strip, Albufeira

Evening.
Stuttering flashes of neon shatter the eyes
iridescent pinks and high-viz oranges
pulsating against the rhythm of techno pop, soul, hiphop
a yellow brick road, a cobbled highway of moons
broken by doorways of light, archways sentried by touts
waving cards of culinary hieroglyphics
wicker chairs, high gloss tables, football screens
replicated prisms on mirrored walls.
Fairground Bronco Billies ride on patios
dodgems spin, bronzed boys from Skegness
raise pints at girls in white lace teetering in spangled heels.
Young policemen idle by the crossroads
wild lions, watching the procession of girls
and couples, kids and Granma, stalls of leather
and jewellery where the guys from the Ivory Coast
settle back in folding chairs, filming the night
with their blanket eyes.

Fox

Across the road from St Joseph's, summer had arrived
with its heady scent and a proliferation of bees.
Greenery ran the length of the fence, an overspill
of shoots and vines, thorns and Queen Anne's lace.
The railway track shunts overhead, highspeed through
the last wild space of foxglove and nettles where
suddenly he appeared as if he had been beamed there
transmigrated from another world, radiating a luminous
glow in the undergrowth. We both stood still, I
with the race of traffic behind me, transfixed by his cub
gaze that held no fear, only curiosity of the kind one
encounters whilst walking country paths and cliffs
compelled to acknowledge the stranger approaching
you through the broom.

Wellington Crescent, Ramsgate, 1973

This is not our house. We are sheep folded
into the flock. Landing in Babylon, my mother
sought a priest who pleaded with his parish
for rooms, furniture, beds for a new immigrant
with four daughters. We are on the third floor,
there are staircases to climb. Some tenants
have a balcony. We haven't got a balcony
but we can look out at the sea through large
sash windows. This is the English Channel.
Its colour changes through the day from murky
brown to almost black to sequinned jewels
dancing on the water. There is the Port of
Ramsgate. Millionaires dock their millionaire
yachts in the harbour. We know nothing of
this town, Regency? Victorian? The rich retired
for their health. Ramsgate is part of a trio, Margate,
Broadstairs, collectively known as The Isle of Thanet.
We know nothing of Dunkirk, of Vikings or Saxons.
They taught us about Henry and his wives, King
Alfred and his cakes and oh so many wars of spice
and roses. In school the black boys were silent
when they learnt how they got there. But we
are foreign now and we're always being asked
where we came from.

Bill Lewis

Bill Lewis was one of the six Medway Poets, a founder member of The Stuckists, and winner of the 2012 Literature Award from the Medway Culture and Design Award. He is a former Writer in Residence at the Brighton Festival. He has performed his poetry in the USA, Nicaragua, Germany, France and in his native UK. His work has been broadcast on TV and Radio including Radio Faribundo Marti in El Salvador, BBC 2, Radio Alice Springs and in the USA. His work has been translated into German, Italian, Spanish and French.

Moon Hare

Moon-full and still a little March-mad
Under the first full moon of April
The brown hare made white by
                                        reflected luna light

A stolen crucifix in its mouth, trailing
Rosary beads behind it like debris
In a comet's tail as it dashes through

The long grass, fast in fear that the moon
Lady might split its lip with a silver axe.

Alhambra

In this palace poised between
Water and infinity, where even
The air is covered in
                    Arabic calligraphy,
A strange and mysterious
Mathematics circumvents
Logic, where seven and four do
Not equal eleven but One.
In its ceilings four is the number
By which the firmament can
Be divided and on its walls
We are told of the seven layers
Of paradise the soul must travel.
All this points to the One
From which all numbers flow

Apple Pickers 1940

for Marge and Arthur Earl

As they work, above them a
Spitfire takes on a Messerschmitt.

The daily dog fights of the
Autumn days of nineteen forty.

The Spit like a great broken
Bird comes down in the orchard.

The wicker baskets fall from
Their hands, apples bruising
On wet grass as they rush to help.

They pull the pilot free from
The fuselage, he is just nineteen.

At first they think him wounded
But it is just the red hydraulic fluid.

Marge is a Land Girl and
Arthur a Reservist waiting to be

Called up. This is how they met.
It was a fruit picker's morning.

Pockets of mist in the valley.
The river Medway a white snake.

Estragon and Vladimir Have left the Theatre

Godot finally got there but
Estragon and Vladimir were gone.

Put another book upon the fire
I'm getting cold, I'm getting on.

Godot was always very tardy
Estragon and Vladimir: mere
Existential Laurel and Hardy.

Obvious meaning makes me mean,
I find it just gets in the way.

Estragon and Vladimir now wait
Far away while Godot's here to stay.

Jasper Summer

Dumbledores bumble about
The lavender and lion's teeth,

An upturned glass upon the
Table a Jasper trapped beneath.

When I get up to leave I will
Lift his prison; let him buzz free.

I try not to harm annoying insects
Be they wasp or be they bee.

Dumbledore = Kentish for bumble bee
Jasper = Kentish for wasp
Lion's teeth = dent-de-lion
Norman French for a Dandelion

Planes

Extract from Masques

The *crema* on the surface of a black coffee.
The distant borborygmus traffic that is
Always somewhere off stage; in the wings.
Rain patters on the window while simultaneously
In the unopened notebook on the table, it is a
Summer day in a different country and the only
Noise emanates from hosts of cicadas.
The two planes slide and intersect, and I am not
On either of them, as at the moment I'm standing
In an eighteen-year-old body at the centre of
A snow-covered field in the village of my youth,
Smoking a cigar and wearing too much aftershave
(both being presents given to me on Christmas day)
This younger me is imagining the future as this older
Me is imagining the past, wondering where I
Actually am, the *who*, the *what* and the *why* of me.
The three planes slide together, and I return.
Our atmosphere, I am told, is the depth
Of a breath misting the surface of a glass marble
The *crema* on the surface of a black coffee.

Extract from **Marginalia**

In The Book of the Hours of the Virgin,
A bored looking nun picks penises from
A phallus tree, piling her wicker basket
Full of strange fruit as if they were
Nothing more than apples and pears.
She will labour for centuries imprisoned;
Marginalised, until the ink fades on the
Vellum, the harvest never to be consumed.

The Pre-History of Genetic Engineering

The Ice Age bit down hard
Game was scarce so the
Wolves helped the humans
To hunt and then hung around
Afterwards for their share.
A man threw one of the wolves
Some cooked meat and the
Wolf entered his magnetic
Influence; A quadruped planet
Orbiting a bipedal star.
The man said, *trust me* and
The wolf woke up in the
Body of a dachshund, in
The form of a chihuahua
Fetch the stick. Fetch the stick.
Moral: Never trust anyone
Who walks on two legs
They'll make you look stupid.

Coyote Poem: Grand Theft Auto

Something tricky in the cosmos,
Something with pointy ears,

Something with a long nose,
Something with a ragged tail,

Something that steals your chickens,
Something that hot wires your car.

I'm talking Grand Theft Auto,
I'm talking Grand Theft Auto.

Something that drives a
Stolen *Thunderbird* across the
Red Martian desert of the New Mexico
Badlands and smiles at you from the
Glossy cover of *Arizona Highways*.

Something that runs over a
Roadrunner on Route 66.
Beep beep now, you little bastard
I said beep beep now.

The Gender of Time is Black

The gender of time is black.
I am caught up in her dance.
She wears a necklace of clocks.
From a distance they look
          like human skulls.

A man paints his feelings
But instead we see a cornfield,
Where crows are startled
By the yellow hue of a sudden
                    gunshot.

The epileptic sun has an
Iron spike driven into its head.

The colour of time is female.

Flags

You are the flag that I raise,
The lion and the unicorn of me
With their wars of white bread
With their battles of brown bread.
My eye and my hand are the
Emblems of inner insurgencies
That foment revolution against
The tedious tyrannies of the ego.
You are the flag that I raise.
The *Magen David* of my once
starless night and
The crescent moon and star
Of my thousand and one nights,
You are the flag that I raise,
The hammer and sickle of my
Immature idealism and the
Black swastika of my shadow.
You are the flag that I raise,
The *red red rose* of my inclination:
You are the jack of my union
Billowing in the breeze of
Our many meetings and flying
At half-mast when we part.

Poem for Cristina Hoyos

Your frown is a question mark
Disguised as an exclamation,
Between your eyes that are slits in
A beautiful furnace of a face.

You dance, wearing a blouse
Stained with the blood of a ghost,
Between mountains of scrap metal.
Your body is an ingenious device
Translating Andalusian clichés
Into Iberian hyper-realties

Your heel hits the ground and the
Duende rises, riding the shockwave
Of that stamp as it arches over the
Steel and satin curve of your calf,
Rippling up through a thigh that is
The exact shape and dimension of
An afternoon in august and stabbing
Into your sex like a dagger of sound.

You dance wearing a blouse
Stained with the blood of a ghost
Among washing lines where
Bed sheets lines and pillow cases
are pegged, caressed by the wind
like the sails of ancient armadas
Oh Cristina who is not Carmen.
Who is more charismatic than Carmen.

I wish I were dust on your shoes

I wish I were dust
                        on your shoes
I would blow
                        in the air
Fall on your flesh
                        settle on your surfaces.
I would lie like
                        stockings on your
Naked legs;
                        like fake tan
                        on your bare arms.
I wish I were dust
                        on your shoes
I'd seep into every
                        crevice of you;
Even the pores
                        of your skin
would contain
                        powdered poet.

Inca Moonshot

The good ship *Santa Maria* dry docks in a
Dry bay by a dry Sea of Tranquillity,
Having first, without knowing it, cleared the
Sensuous curve of the Earth's gentle hip and
Fallen into the here-be-dragons-dark
of black airless history.
Captain Christopher Columbus still thinks
he has reached the coast of Cathay.

He scans the horizon with a brass telescope,
Not realising he is looking down the wrong
End; he sees in the distance, like angels cut
From tin foil, blonde blue eyed astronauts
Rounding off a game of golf. Behind them on a
flag pole *Old Glory* unflutters in a windless sky.

Neither the sea captain nor the *gringo* space men
Realise that they were not
the first to venture here.
Long before the invention of the sailing ship,
Long before all the Apollo missions,
The people of the under developed world
Walked the Lunar surface by the
sacred technology
Of song, dream and visions, or simply
by calling her Grandmother.
They left no footprints, they walked lightly
(as they did upon the Earth).
They took no part in the Space Race, in which
The USA and the USSR jointly held last place.

A War Of Flowers

For Claribel and Bud

In another America where
The memory is a war of flowers.
Behind the curtain of silence
Rests a grey heat heavier than iron.
Where the red jaguar reclines
And the blue tiger of prophecy
Smashes the world to bits
With a mighty war club of
Lilies and golden orchids.
Shattering the night and using
The shards of its darkness to
Reconstruct the morning,
Luminous with lakes
                                        and lepidoptera.
Devalued are the old currencies
Of chocolate and emerald feathers.
A steel cough hacks at our
External lungs: the trees
The General crushes a gardenia
In the palm of his leather glove.
The Cardinal blesses birdcages
Brass bands, baseball games and
Endless parades of paper petals
The memory is a war of flowers,
A bloody war of flowers.
In another America where
The helicopter gunship desecrates
The azure robe of the mountains
Where the only *mariachis* are
Orchestras of skeletons playing
Their ribcages like *marimbas.*

The Last Poem

You have these dreams where you find a door in
our house that was not there before. You open it
and find a room you have never noticed until now,
despite living there for the last thirty years. I know
you have these dreams because you've told me
about them. Sometimes the room is full of ornate
furnishings, sometimes treasure. Well, when I'm
gone, that is where you'll find me. There, and
only there, in that room behind your eyes. If, by
some chance, I'm not there (I may be visiting
dead friends) in that room on a table there will be
a poem. I'll put it in an envelope and write your
name on it so that you will be sure that it is for
you. Please read it. When you do read it you'll
wonder, typically, the name of the beautiful woman
who inspired it, never guessing it was you. I say
this because I know you so well. Read it again
carefully and remember how I always looked at
you and how you could see what you really looked
like in the mirror of my eyes.

Sarah Hehir

Sarah Hehir is a poet and playwright from the industrial north. Her plays explore and expose abuse of power, shifting the control of the narrative away from authority and giving voice to marginalised individuals and communities. Her poems are about love, life and death. Since winning the inaugural BBC Writer's Prize in 2013, she has written for stage, radio, TV and film.

Glass Half

Mum brought her kazoo to Zoom.
She dragged her bed into the garden
to hear the blackbirds in the morning:
cooked a trout on a fire,
fished from the bottom of the freezer.

Kept her distance.

Tripped over a riddle
and told us it was nothing
even though her wrist was broken.
Wrote a letter to my uncle
so his dying wasn't sterile.
Made a rainbow out of gingham.

Przemyśl Train Station

Have you ever carried a tired child to bed?
Her head rests heavy on your shoulder.
Careful n ot to wake her,
you balance
like a bad ballerina
to toe back the covers
and lower her gently down.

Have you ever carried a screaming child home?
It's all gone wrong.
She's thrashing on the frosty tarmac
between the Post Office and the Co-Op.
You scoop her up,
which is a feat ,
and hold her wriggling weight
as the shopping slips
and one egg breaks.
You fail to soothe her
with her favourite songs.
Her screaming is resolve-breaking.
Her face is fury red.
You swap her from hip to hip,
suggest a piggyback,
almost give up.
But, key in lock, you make it.
No-one will hear your shaky breath
or see your tear smeared face
as you rush to put on Peppa Pig.

Have you ever carried a frightened child across a border?
Seven families do not know but can imagine
the horrors they can't stop from happening.
They can't help with the stone in her stomach
or the ache in her heart
but they can help with the weight in her arms.
On a station platform,
seven empty buggies stand.

Iris Is Not A Cross Country Runner

But she's fierce and fast and tenacious
and so she's selected.

Number 842 is attached
to the front of her red Medway vest
with borrowed pins.
Her tackies from Sports Direct
can't compete with cross country racers.

She knows no-one and won't warm up.
Instead she invents a method
where muscles are shocked into action
by being forced to run
when they least expect it.
She makes me laugh.
I make her want to die
by taking out a sandwich
to eat while we're waiting.

Whistles are blown and they line up.
There's rules:
instructions for starting.
This is a different league from the school field
and Iris suddenly looks small:
less like my bold, brash girl.
She stands pale and cold and still
amongst the jiggling club runners
in their thermal base layers.

The starting whistle sets them off
and they fly across frozen mud ruts
and flat winter grass.
Straight away, I lose her in the mass of legs
and remember what she said about
how her body will blame her
for such a pointless waste
of flight or fight.

I trail after the other mums and dads
who know about times and terrain.

When Iris emerges from
the bony Baba Yaga fingers
of a blackthorn bush,
I wave and cheer.
Her mortified frown hides a smile
before she disappears.

I grin and then
have to stop myself from crying.
I don't know why.
She's fine.
But standing at the finish line,
I just can't wait to see her.

Old Speckled Hen

To sip is to hold back;
drink deep.
Take the flat and ferrous
and savour it.
Take the red skies
of Scunthorpe's steel
and the flat river fields.
Drink it all in

The U-Boat And The Whale

Undercurrent echoes of living flesh
sing through half-sunken subs:
sounds that, leaving Lincolnshire
and heading south, bounce around
The Wash, the Yarmouth Coast,
towards Sheerness.

In search of – what?
A rusty skeleton?

She hears his hunger songs and sings to him
with metal tongue, her own
'Ich weiß es nicht.'

Her iron coffin voice –
depth charged, displaced –
rides north on winter waves.

She waits.
Then tries again.

Wo sind Sie jetzt?

Mud banks and hostile sands.

With ferrous blood in ferrous veins
and heavy heart,
she waits.

Cider Season

The apple that tastes
of slow days of sun,
sweetened by languid kisses
smudged red on pale flesh
and scented with
impossible morning mists,
that apple's fleeting season
is too soon gone;
best to stick to
the cold harsh nip
of a Granny Smith.

The Wrecking Season

Cold wind whips up the winter waves
and sends sea fret to seek me out
in rippled dunes of salty grass
where I lay low beneath dark skies
and only Cornish sucker fish
look up to see me cry.

And This Is Not The End Of You

First softer sounds
thrum through synapses,
then breaking waves soak the
lyrical land,
lilting to the quick of you,
bitter and beautiful.

You turn your back
but that languid language
takes wayward ways around
and snags at time
and holds onto you:
emerging or escaping.

The wrecking tide
leaves ghostly shapes,
desolate somewhere and
so long love-lost;
a beach, a boat,
a place, a man.
A life unlived in.

The whispered threat
cuts silence through its
cold, shell shaped echoing,
leaving a clue;
a solid ink imprint.
Who are you?
What might you do?

Going Outside In The Middle Of The Night

Log Pile	oak and silver birch
Feet	bare
Fig Tree	unplanted
	one lonely fig
	on stark stick
	with tinsel twist
	and fox gift tag
Dog Bowl	half full
	with slow silver trail
	of snail, roaming
Dead geranium	in frost cracked pot
Wind	fresh
	woody
	storm blown
Trees	dark
Clouds	scudding
Sky	high
	studded with stars
	that act like drawing pins
	for strings
	attaching me
	to infinity
	like a desolate marionette

The Weight Of Antony

Stands he or sits he?
She wonders which
as she lies naked, asp-gasping,
beneath Egyptian sheets:
the king of cottons,
fit for a queen.

Or is he on his horse?
A skin memory
of soldier's thighs,
muscle-bound, rippling in khaki combats,
commanding his steed
with deep battle cries.

Oh happy horse
Her own hands slip over breast and belly,
skin burnished gold and bathed in honey.
She longs for him with stallion envy,
fills the love-sick wind with cherries.
Calls for cyanide and venom.

I Stand: Useless Stranger

A small girl
kneels outside the pharmacy
and vomits quietly
from a stomach, already empty,
into the snow that sticks to Canterbury Street.

Her mum,
knees of her jeans wet,
holds the girl's hair back,
pulling out tissues from anorak pockets
and whispering words to keep the girl safe
and to keep the girl warm.

I offer my help, my hand, my scarf.
Her mum shakes her head.
She doesn't need my stuff but she takes the hug
like a gust of love from the cut of the cold
and we both lean in.

She's scared, she says, of another long night,
afraid and alone with her shadow-eyed child
and only the promise
of waiting lists and waiting lines,
of online forms and GP calls
and A&E as a last resort.

I nod to the mum and the girl
and wish them good luck and mutter goodbye.
Thank you, her mum says with a sigh.
Luck is all you have if you're cold
and sick and only a kid.

When No Storm Comes

I steal through secret morning streets
with no excuse – no work no exercise,
just the need to feel the pinch of night

before morning's harsh reality throws light,
like a blinding spot, on troubled times.
This city is not mine.

Cove Point

The Black Feathers
scribble invisible ink letters
to long lost lovers
across the furthest arcing reaches
of the textured off-white sky.

For My Valentine

Just left of darkness,
our soon sleeping
shapes are licked
by night’s blank face.

Barry Fentiman Hall

Barry Fentiman Hall is a Medway based poet from the north. He has been published across a diverse range of journals in the UK, Ireland, and North America, including Crack The Spine, Anti-Heroin Chic, International Times, Lit Quarterly (Canada), Ink Sweat & Tears, The Cormorant, Dreich, The Journal, Seaside Gothic, Marble, and Picaroon. His three collections The Unbearable Sheerness Of Being, England, My Dandelion Heart, and Sketches are all available from Wordsmithery.
As part of Wordsmithery he is currently the editor of Confluence Magazine, and the co-director of both Rainham Poetry Festival and Medway River Lit.

Adventures in Sound

What if the tapping at the window was not a raven?
Poe's true love may have been throwing grit to get his attention
She waited for him in the snow night after night
but he was convinced it was a raven and they never met

The cars on the by-pass become eroticised by the moon
There seem to be so many more of them than there used to be
Their irregular breathing like lovers making out in a lay-by
Nyloned legs keeping time
                    as they walk away throwing the keys in a ditch
Or maybe it's just me that listens for such things
                    where they don't exist

Brian Wilson had an orchestra in his head
                              playing at different speeds
The bells fell behind the drums and came home after dark
The audience talked among themselves
                              and became part of the show
He can still hear them when the music ends
They never stop talking

My father can still speak when I open my mouth unguarded
He sighs when I get to the top of the stairs at work
As I hum the scarecrow's song
                         that never played when it should have
but never stops playing for me
                         in the spaces in between my dreams

I am convinced that I can hear people's hearts beating far away
Sometimes they skip a little when life gets big on them
The needle jumps drawing mountains
                              that may really be mountains
Although it is possible that my ears are playing up
                              and it's my own heart that has stopped

England Forgets

England forgets and gets loose
On scuffed golden fields of wilt and weeds
It bares its back and shows its best side to the sky

Pleading the beams to fall a little longer
Mizzed by rain for long months
We get baked high on heat

And we love each other
With an honesty that cannot be bottled
And kept for when the clouds return

We are knocking back the now
A song we know is the breath of trees
We take it way back and laugh at anything

Not embarrassed to embrace, we part
Slow till only fingers tip, and let go
Walking like myths on familiar streets

At midnight, that smell of honeysuckle
Or some such, longing out the high
We glow still for a while

Until the heat leaves us, and life goes on
As England remembers itself
With half a smile, until the next time

England, My Dandelion Heart

Oh England, my dandelion heart
What have you done with that cross that you carved?
A horde of golden fools, marching the meadow

Did you believe it marked the spot?
An X Factor expedition, seeking riches that will
always remain the other side of the screen

Oh my England! A grasping scar that
you have made across a land that
could have been greener and more pleasant

Now so far away it seems
This lion now has lost its teeth
Whipped dogs they are

Digging for something they do not know they need
So what do they think they'll find down there?
A bigger car? An empire? Eldorado? An avocado?

Or the knowledge plain and simple that
they haven't hit the bottom yet - Oh England, my dandelion heart
That dream that I am clinging to

Now ploughed beneath the muck of suburban dreamers'
avaricious digging - bowing down they scratch with a mug of
schadenfreude to match

All in it together, pressed and serried
Though all they'll find I fear
Is where the bodies are buried.

Fruit Picking

For Don & Gloria Phillips

We berry on the Coney Banks that back the old fort
Where they paper the walls of the museum café
with holiday posters of rouged flappers wanting
young lads for fruit picking
In other orchards
across the sea from here

Where the ring of concrete sleeps apples hang on crabby trees
lost beyond the wire, caught up, leaning at an angle
The fattest always sweeting just beyond our certain reach
Scrubby underfoot and steep
Falling from our grasp like bodies
on the far off playing fields

Boys played their games on foreign ground,
schooled, across the cinder path, saying things their brothers said
Not taking third light mate
Soft mouths cough at the bitter taste of hearsay things to come
When they'd suck the pear and share blood
with the late glow harvest sun

Buried on the Coney Banks, rising roots catch our feet
Here goes youth in peace preserved like damson jam
Lessons learned, homework forgot
Factors, multiples, and primes trod, gone to the eternal next
Repeating years, like old boys when they were small
who were never going to lose the war

The Road To Domestos

Paul lands upon my shoulder, his eyes as great and grey as moths
He turns gravely slow, to see that the door has closed behind him

It clicks and he sits and gazes at the letters that I feed
He marvels at the speed and tries to count them as they

Flutter by to Sevenoaks or some such, we pass some time
With nods and smiles and warmly offered words that trickle dry

In the hot fast world beyond him, soft he sets off with little sighs
To push his bin and wipe some tiles
He wasn't always this they say

The boy that was born, got lost in the fog one day
On the road to Domestos, his changeling face a poster child
Asking for information, that may bring him back
We found him once in a quiet place, spinning a cocoon

Till the doctor came, to stroke his wings and sing to him
It happens now and then
they say

Incident Suite

I - Albert Road

There's no croissants today, or pecan Danish
The woman in pyjamas who came for her dailies
will have to sweat and wait
Like the bananas that sit outside on plastic trays

There's a hole in the roof over the counter
where the fags and the booze all vanished out of
Cheap bare boards that the boot went through
the muck under the polish

Dint think they were clever enough round here to think of that
Said Pyjamas, impatient in the teatime beer queue
PC Broadley needs sleep as she shifts her feet
Guarding the crime scene with a flat thin smile
A line on her face you'd be advised not to cross
this side of Friday night

Merlin House drips light like water
Heat, casting lustre on stones
wet with night; open like a passion flower
Brighter than rain
The chef saw nothing through the thickdrip windows

And the thin young fox smiles it seems
as she grows vixen
Fleeting low behind next door's Mercedes
Knows something; she is witness but keeps it zipped
and takes what she needs fearless of being seen

II - Southill Road

There's no crossing the road today, redirected
I sweat and wait, exhaling from the climb
Steam from my breath
lifting, mixing with the dank laundry drift

PC Broadley huffs doing the gutter shuffle
Waving not drowning, she can do this all day
I crossed the line, jogged, got by her
Big lad hi-viz, holds the trailer
Where you going mate? Home, down there...
Lets me hop over and away

There's a hole in the wing of the squad car
Crumpled like a bashed cake, iced crumbs spread
across the pavement, where the Audi hit
Three hurt they said

Elis lads rub shoulders, sing, off shift in scrubs
They banter lasses' Spice Girl harmonies
Ears ringing, heads light
Brows wet with work
They saw nothing through the starless windows

The proud fox runs, big now, licks lips
Grown full vixen
Taking bones brazen by the Uma shop
Knows everything; witness to the world unfurled
Has grown to fear it, but she will be seen

III – Wetherspoons

There's no use pretending it's the rain
The queue for the library gets shorter daily
We sit at our desks, eat biscuits, and wait
while sanitized fingers catch up with emails

There are pools of old fluids ringing the counter
as I decompress after work with cheap craft bitter
Sensitized to Birch pollen I sneeze violently
You just got back from China mate?
shouts aleface husband already turned
doing the walk away dance giggling with wifey

PC Broadley types up reports of shop rage
wearing evidence gloves to much derision
from colleagues who will be off sick by Friday
A wise move when using sticky keys

The sound of one man coughing has been heard
on every television in the world
Maidstone and Faversham make the news
People interviewed know nothing
Self isolating prophecies come true
No pubs, no gyms, just social distancing

The foxes go about their business
immune to human troubles
Evolved to go from home to home
licking clean the chicken bones
now the streets are theirs

IV – Symons Avenue

There's no getting past it, people are angry
Passive aggression sweats on the pavement
heavy, in sport-smart shabbed at the cuffs
Ragged from the slog of having to
Exaggerated hands waving through

There's a stand-off outside Greenvale School
Engines idle, heads of drivers rev hot breath,
hands on wheel whiting on the clock
Black face faces white face, anxious kid faces
sit in back seats, wanting tea and TV
and Tom Hardy telling a story

PC Broadley sits at home feet fluffed
mug in hand not fussed watching Countdown
as a mother hauls descending kids
last one wailing like a siren
far away, always distant

It's always terrible down here at this hour
she says to no-one in particular
Dragging her good times behind her,
trailing like a row of cars behind a shaking fist
Resigned to all of this

The old fox is dead now, after
gone under wheels her truth spoken,
expectancy of life achieved,
Cold under decorum's wood
A found coffin soaks her blood
and a teenage couple's nervous laughter

V- A2*

Knuckle push of button pointless
as great space sweeps up 4 lanes
Quiet now in lockdown peace
The way it was in the before times
In the distance shiver tales in tapes

Measured by matchstick figures
Taraxacum gold scratches grey
All unfolds in that, draws eye
Distances are being weighed
ready for the incisive verdict

PC Broadley gone, no honour guard
Did her job, the gob and spit
of rub-eye Friday nights on shift
Younger than she looked in blues
Forever that, and never clapped

Pushed back drive to work too soon
Surfing the wave in rear view
Tapping wheels hyperflexible
Can't sit still, collar twitches tight
Contraflow calm in throbbing tin

I saw the flowers dead and bright
Haring spray luminous in amber
mumble something drinker sees me
capture the scene, no fox comes
Rain does, like fine earth in eulogy

*previously unpublished

A Lay Bye For Lucid Dreamers

Soft traffic sounds in dust and water
Hanging where the city runs away
With the dreams its people once had
That flow like cut wrists in the bath

But it doesn't have to be like that
When the bypass sings to us
Lost loving lucid and forbidden
We throw the sticks and make the beat

The sand falls like cars on the shum
Metronoming in the far places ending
Where the mind stops for a burger
Fried in three o' clock special sauce

We get the spice buzz on ticking seeds
Of doubt coated in hot hope on hard shoulders
We can hear them going places, out there
Till we begin to dream in motion

They fade, and we are driving easy
Riding, white lining in the half place
Where the road runs out and remembers
What was there long before the metaling

We are earth before the buttered black
Melting like clocks set for seven am
Falling asleep at the wheel, yearning
For a place we cannot find again.

The Elder On The 164

Beyond the arches the hill bus runs
Bumping the ruts   like an old cart
Spilling chickens from plague Europe
Carrying up peasants to a feast day hanging

We are all manner of blotchy flesh tones
The pallid and the grey and many shades
From blue to black - Pieter Bruegel
The Elder looks on bearded at the back

In his too big biker jacket sketching
great noses on startled looking women
in archetypal headscarves, lulling
their grandchildren on mighty bruised knees

As the great wheels turn past gibbets
standing crows for the eyes of the elder
His metaphor of truth or maybe just birds
We are thinning now, our destinations reached

White roads provoke a shuffling
of sticks and baskets - this land
of prescription Cockaigne
is the place that we call home

Under Speeton Cliffs, 3am, January 1990

My memories of Speeton beach at night are sleet shaped

Pain thrown from the dead black beyond the lamp

A seahowl that asks to touch me

To divine me like a blind preacher

My face in its cold hands

Checking my teeth

I cannot explain my trespass at eight pence a worm

Korevaar is fleet for a man of twenty stone

Picking off the gasping clams

Spade lashed to his massive back

Gravecasts wold in his wake, he cuts deeper than other men

Tindall nithers in his tracks

Done to stone, a body gone to shakes

Tyler claps the time we dance to

Doublebook twister he

Gobby till mammy skins him blind

and leaves him coppershare for ale

I'll have mine even if she blacks me

Razor clams cannot breathe when the sand freezes

I know how they feel these nights

Baited,

ready for the hook

The Woman Who Talked To Herself

My mother worked in the factories
She could lip read as a matter of course
All self-taught
As the hazelnut whirls filed past
on the packing conveyor at Terry's
Filling her ears with white noise and cocoa dust

She would show off this special skill at the garden gate
Her and Reeny Charlton
With me at her knee
When the conversation turned to ladies matters
About who'd had what done
And who'd given who what for
Their mouths would move meaningfully
but no words would come out

Much later, half deaf, long after the rollers had stopped
And Chocolate Oranges were picked in Poland
She began to mouth at the air silently
As though tasting it for sugar
A mischievous smile and a movement of the shoulders
That thing she did when knowing what we didn't
In her old chair at the old house
Before we shipped her off to be looked after

We sat chatting there in her little room
About times I could not remember
About brothers, others, and maybe lovers
And eventually her mother, Mystery Lyd
Who worked the kitchens serving chips
Before Ma had to call it home

And it was then she called me Betty
Casting her breath on a mirror
Obscuring the past for the sake of the boy

Missing being a twin perhaps
To a child you cannot explain that loss
Silently singing the remembrance song
Staying strong on chocolate Sundays
Yes, she was talking to herself
And it is not a boy's business
To know who she thought she was

1972 Deconstructed/Reconstructed

Lyd was my grandmother
  Lydia Mary Teesdale/Teasdale 1910-1972
Glasses, dyed hair, cig lit
  The spelling seemed to be optional
That's how I remember her
  Even the war office weren't certain
A crow regarding me
  Seen off two husbands by then
Pale thought in a nightgown
  But not the rumours about the others

I was about three then
  BFH b1969
At the foot of her bed
  Maybe I had been brought in
Studying my face, for traces
  To say goodbye
Of something, she never said
  I am honestly not sure
Beady; corvid quizzical
  Exactly what she looked like

She never spoke to me
  She must have said something
That I can certainly recall
  That's the trouble with early memories
One day I would have this room
  I slept in this room
From this time, 1972
  From the time she died
Until my brother left home
  Till about 1980

I was dreaming of a future
I could have been dreaming about anything
When girls could stay over
It was more likely football, at least to start with
Which in that bed one did
Much later, after an awkward chat with dad
Oblivious to Lyd's presence
I am assuming the mattress had been changed
As a family ghost of sorts
But I don't want to think about that

Was she smoking still?
Probably, everyone did then
Or wearing a shroud of fine morning mist
Probably not, though that room was very cold
Foretelling death approaching
Used to get ice inside the windows
As the recollections of my childhood
Which Lydia am I recalling?
So often seem to be
With the "e", with the "a", or the one I made up?

I do not believe in spirits
I am sure that I could find photographs
Or have faith in memory
Of Lydia if I looked hard enough
The mind and the eye
But what would be the point now?
Are unreliable senses
It would spoil all this fine imagery
And writers fill in the gaps
That I used to fill in the gaps

Rainsnow

Soft flakes fall like cannon shots across delta Sunday rooftops

Prompting panicked questions from gathering workshoppers

It's pitching says Samantha, as they do out West

where it hardly even snows

throwing a scarf about her neck

Before the heat of my cheek is lost from her embrace

And so she goes, bags in tow, a galaxy of talents

to take to the printers table,

being far too good about my absence

So I remain behind, mummified, dancing with the duvet

in a fever of guilt and bacteria

and the never ending rows of artists

Call me in a thousand years   Leave a message under the stone

Me and Morpheus have an understanding, he lets me sleep

if he can write my dreams, the sand flows like salt into a wound

He won't let me forget a single thing, makes me start awake

Coughing dust from my stitched mouth

The tablet is   broken

A last message   The doctor will see you now

The outside world is melting, so I must become a thing of it

To breathe its creeky air I am rainsnow running cold

In Byron's silted gutter, lost among the memories

  Of poets with a pocketful of opoids

        This drowned place shivers

But it warms me, this river, slips me laudanum for the soul

The hospital express is lit like a sorry Christmas lantern

For me alone to read by, scanning the features of cafe society

In the scattered leaves that blew far from familiar trees

  They are good company, these lives

        On this unheroic journey home

It didn't pitch then says Samantha,

            as I rest my cold cheek against her

Acknowledgements

Maggie Harris:
Some of these poems have been published in previous collections: *Foreday Morning, Limbolands, From Berbice to Broadstairs, After a Visit to a Botanical garden, 60 Years of Loving, On Watching a Lemon Sail the Sea.* 'Goa' will be published in her next collection; *I sing to the Greenhearts.*

Photograph © Eleanor Marriot

Bill Lewis:
Poem for Cristina Hoyos, I Wish I Were the Dust On Your Shoes, Flags, The Last Poem, From In The House of Ladders – Greenheart Press 2012
The Gender of Time is Black, Alhambra – From The Long Ago and Eternal Now – Greenheart Press 2017
Moon Hare, Coyote Poem: Grand Theft Auto, Inca Moonshot, A War of Flowers – From This Love Like a Rage Without Anger – Colony Press 2019
Apple Pickers, 1940, Etragon and Vladimir Have Left The Theatre, Jasper Summer, Planes, Marginalia, The Pre-History of Genetic Engineering From Sparrowhawk – Colony Press 2022

Photograph © Emma Dewhurst/Greenheart Press

Sarah Hehir:
The Weight of Anthony, This is not the end of you From Assembly of Judicious Heretics Poems - Wordsmithery
U-boat and the Whale From 23 Submarines
The Wrecking Season From Fiction Magazine

Photograph © Nicola Maund

Barry Fentiman Hall:
1972 Deconstructed-Reconstructed - first published in The Lit Quarterly 5 (Canada) 2021
Adventures In Sound - England, My Dandelion Heart - Wordsmithery 2018
England Forgets - England, My Dandelion Heart - Wordsmithery – 2018
England, My Dandelion Heart - England, My Dandelion Heart - Wordsmithery – 2018
Fruit Picking - Sketches - Wordsmithery – 2020
Rainsnow - England, My Dandelion Heart -Wordsmithery 2018
Incident Suite – All from Sketches - Wordsmithery – 2020
Lay Bye For Lucid Dreamers - The Blue Nib 39 Sept 2019
The Elder on the 164 - England, My Dandelion Heart - Wordsmithery – 2018
The Woman Who Talked To Herself - Marble Issue 7 2020
Under Speeton Cliffs 3am January 1990 - Seaside Gothic Issue 1 – 2021
The Road To Domestos - England, My Dandelion Heart - Wordsmithery – 2018

Photograph: © Neil Thorne Photography

Milton Keynes UK
Ingram Content Group UK Ltd.
UKHW010948050224
437294UK00004B/216